ADVANCED PRAISE FOR
A NET OF MOMENTARY SAPPHIRE

"A net is a texture for catching" Samuel Johnson says in his dictionary, which I have gone to for help in finding words for the singular and moving experience of reading this poem-length book. Both thing and process, Kolewe's net is formed from precise tercets and the irregular gaps between them, glittering, resurging, sinking, swaying, and reappearing in a baroque pattern of strangeness. What this recurrent weave catches is the faceted flickering of linguistic consciousness within the reader's melodic attention. We read, we're always the same reader, and we're also the reader who is about to be fundamentally changed by a turning page. Kolewe's metaphysical verse poses itself entirely and generously in the difficult movement of this continuing present by means of an ethical delicacy knotted from threads of tradition, doubt, and the acutely sensual rendering of daily perception. It holds astonishing beauty.

—LISA ROBERTSON
  author of *Boat* and *The Baudelaire Fractal*

There's an eerily familiar ambivalence to the means by which *A Net of Momentary Sapphire* keeps circling, keeps turning over what it's trying to grasp. Its visions and revisions are tensioned by the potential for the absolutely meaningful – for getting it just right, for the singular phrase – versus the epic experience of not quite making it there. As Kolewe quietly unfurls the myriad, crippling richness of multiplying possibilities, somehow the elusiveness of really knowing, of unequivocal sense-making, speaks the search for meaning into radiance all while recording its shortfalls. It's a painfully alive book that entangles a reader over and over again.

—DAVID BRADFORD
  author of *Dream of No One but Myself*

A NET OF MOMENTARY SAPPHIRE

ALSO BY R. KOLEWE

The Absence of Zero

Inspecting Nostalgia*

Afterletters

*Published by Talonbooks

A NET OF
MOMENTARY
SAPPHIRE

R. KOLEWE

TALONBOOKS

Talonbooks
9259 Shaughnessy Street, Vancouver, British Columbia, Canada v6p 6r4
talonbooks.com

Talonbooks is located on xʷməθkʷəẏəm, Sḵwx̱wú7mesh, and səlilwətaʔɬ Lands.

First printing: 2023

Typeset in Arno
Printed and bound in Canada on 100% post-consumer recycled paper

Cover and interior design by Typesmith
Cover image by Typesmith

Talonbooks acknowledges the financial support of the Canada Council for the Arts, the Government of Canada through the Canada Book Fund, and the Province of British Columbia through the British Columbia Arts Council and the Book Publishing Tax Credit.

Library and Archives Canada Cataloguing in Publication

Title: A net of momentary sapphire / R. Kolewe.
Names: Kolewe, R. (Ralph), 1957- author.
Identifiers: Canadiana 20220483752 | ISBN 9781772015188 (softcover)
Subjects: LCGFT: Poetry.
Classification: LCC PS8621.O47 N48 2023 | DDC C811/.6—dc23

And these things,
in leaving still living, know that you praise them; transient,
they trust us, the most transient, to be their salvation,
want us, in our unseeable hearts, to transform them totally
into – O unending – into us! Whoever, in the end, we may be.

—RILKE
"The Ninth Elegy"

PART ONE

THE FORETASTE OF A VISION, BUT NEVER THE VISION ITSELF

Once again & innumerable times again
the required solitude, renunciation, strange
curtained doubt artifice all jewelled

& after this

silent time, these days
& nights in desert
dry country, dry thoughts

breathing, strengthening
desolation look closely:
lizard, scorpion, beetle

sky thick with stars, one red star.
Or grey cloud, recalled ashes
unscattered, unclaimed, unaccounted for

& after this

no liturgy. Nothing holy. Ordinary
hours under sun & moonless
night. Unarranged

stones breeding sand,
shadow. No. The moon
comes & goes, some

nights you can't see past sky.
Don't know why it might be
beautiful, whose name goes here

& after this

overhanging rock & waste
where you arrive, where
you're led to. No word what

4

follows stones, pinnacles.
Is it better to say nothing?
No bright images. No books

or too many books,
revised versions.
In every case, empty pages

& after this

nothing else
but a kind of circling.
Mountain flowers

bloom like brocade,
valley streams brimming blue indigo.
On the ancient cliff, frigid juniper.

Nothing written breathes or turns,
every word exiled. Empty
forms between the ivory gates

& after this

because there are no
borders here
because the horizon's

subdued mass is solace, luminous
as if understanding arrives
self-forgotten & entangled

staying alive corrupt as we all are
traceries of flame falling slowly
in a moment of time –

& after this

past closed doors
& no doors despair
the world's untouched small fold

of flesh deserted only
old staging without
chorus without masks

small tough plants & echoes
& memories of rain
the umbrella you wouldn't use

& after this

suffering as humans suffer
hunger lust grief
at this table without prayer or bread

cruel rain in the midst of winter
without remains only
trace minerals isotope

ratios a bit off
banal trauma of ordinary life
not worth remarking

& after this

it should be intent & transparent
here, isn't, is
however passionless, incredulous,

not abandoned enough some
green & crimson called
flowers small winged serpent allure

saying never mind it
can be repaired,
just wait that's what we want to hear

& after this

rain becoming
snow, thickening & slowing
thought concluding

the argument has only one
outcome, historical inevitability,
social construction, truth.

No return from here.
Not meaning.
Not existence.

& after this

no way to escape but that
we find if brought forth
we go on

axe & root, backbone, rue
our medicine, our medium, our meditation
not always

innocence taken, withered,
formerly bounteous tree, in another
weather esteem

& *after this*

if reason failing
runs, all faith left
for quick passions

there is life in them
or nothing but pretending.
No talk of that in this theatre

repentance will turn away.
To the end also
trespass, purpose, cunning

& after this

early life the house empty.
The field.
Wind caryatid scattered.

Descending vector at every point.
Not rain looping.
Not turbulence.

No signature.
No distant figure.
Impure rough-sawn tone

& after this

if only we'd remembered!
Pendant emptiness unmasked sky
one word after another word.

Parentheses, red in black
or beauty out of bounds
red becoming rust quickly.

More than pen scratching fire
can only follow so far the word absent
& not enough silence.

PART TWO

LIKE THE NOISES ALIVE
PEOPLE WEAR

1.

In the next room someone reading stage directions
trying to name the scene familiar foreign
always even what comes next is far away.

No correct one. A branching
tangled tree overgrown with vines, unlined
now. Monochrome, only edges.

2.

The everyday again the everyday.
I don't care about Rilke's angels anymore, I said.
Sweep the floor. Put away the books. Fill a glass with water.

You can't so both you & the world must
be broken. The river shallow in late
summer a net of momentary sapphire.

In sight & higher, the stars, the dead
always suppose we who –
Where? Look, I am living.

3.

That thing they posted Clark Coolidge wrote keep
on writing more or less even
if the room is empty even if the words are empty even

circling around something I don't understand or circling
around nothing (& I don't understand that either)
& that's enough. Well, loss is tiresome yes every day.

4.

Past unravelled though text
remains, read, reread, uncertain
how the one who wrote managed.

Borrowing another poet's words again
only half remembering
it coolly disdains to destroy you.

5.

I can't write what I really can't.
Remember leave things out I am like bees.
That's the real thing is what I said I said.

Ah, but then we would become more than
modern, & death
always so contemporary.

6.

A few words stolen from a stranger ill-met in early fog,
no story at all, even repetition no better self-deception
rewriting the same pages again.

7.

Rework this as there's no joy here
& not enough voices no long poem containing
history –

too many ways to divide all these pages & letters & elegies
archaic forms of life unchanged by notebooks or photographs
or beauty unnameable recognized –

8.

A few words stolen from a stranger ill-met in early fog,
borrowing another poet's words again.
Dust dulling the wood floor in the sunlight.

9.

Not as if starting an inventory like Perec
(notebook, pen, stack of novels, socks, the cat)
(already I'm lying) but overlap or fold or imprecise

rework this as there's no joy here
& not enough voices no long poem containing
history –

10.

The everyday overlaps the extraordinary.
I have no idea what these blue flowers are.
Dust dulling the wood floor in the sunlight.

11.

The whole thing
comes apart without
violence this time.

12.

The everyday overlaps the extraordinary.
I have no idea what these blue flowers are.
Dust dulling the wood floor in the sunlight.

Throwing rocks at what is it downed owl or rabbit or cat
at the back of the schoolyard ditch white with snow & dark
woods beyond look blood it's not moving now –

Maybe this needs a violet resonance, a cadmium ringing, to be
spread out once you might have asked the poem what was right.
You, the poet, someone listening. The cliché.

13.

Even in the city walking
at dawn alone with birdsong
wait I can tell you their names –

No need to start. Too much quiet.
When you.could take one step forward
without thinking envy privilege tradition –

14.

Borrowing another poet's words again
only half remembering
beauty is nothing but the beginning of terror

vision & revision of
every word a new life
again emptied out.

Substance & accident.
Like the colour of road salt or snow.
One melts in your hand. All fall down.

15.

Despite the denial beginning & no slow consideration
why don't they fade away like scars or tail lights trying
not to tell the story again these line breaks don't twist enough –

16.

In sight & higher, the stars, the dead
always suppose we who –
Where? Look, living

dimly not keeping time winding down or burning out
disappointment to be rebuilt as philosophy perhaps
realization or actualization the fundamental inexplicable
    experienced –

17.

The language spoken across the street. Fire
just below the breastbone every breath too aware
of breathing. Fingers cramped, their hold too tight.

18.

This is the desert. The remnant.
Allow yourself one word a day.
That should be enough.

Portraits of strangers just waking. Self-portraits, asleep.
Bedclothes clenched in which radiance & emptiness are indivisible.
Asking the wrong question. Almost-shattered glass.

Despite the denial beginning & no slow consideration
why don't they fade away like scars or tail lights trying
not to tell the story again this line breaks –

19.

Literature piles up to be set aside,
spurious politics & careerism, but the
light, the light, past the first radiance second & the clouds –

20.

Substance & accident.
Like the colour of road salt or snow.
One melts in your hand. All fall down.

No need to start. Too much quiet.
When could you take one step forward
without thinking

what changed, yes, large things, borders & electric light,
consenting to stay buried in a narrow smoky world
absolutes & department stores but writing –

21.

Where validity edges Wednesday
far below, waves on rocks white
prayer ocean as if endless if –

22.

Vision & revision of
every word a new life
again emptied out

even if some of it is singing
& some lines have been
silenced, still

nothing new in it but
every pain & every joy & every thought & sigh & everything
unspeakably small or great in your life.

23.

Like rain, or snow, or lightning, or
the reconstructed track of decaying cosmic rays
never having done this yet.

Those words ritual of those words when
there was no ritual only reading
later & sometimes aloud. Reading to others.

24.

Consumed / as a flame consumes
as a flame consumes
as fire / consumes

undistracted no one cross that out no
action is destroyed & choice
later irrelevant to later –

25.

Nothing modern terrifying or beautiful absence itself
unravels leaving you to follow the thread scarlet or azure
eventually non-local hierarchies though details differ

(climbing cold mountain
the phone in your pocket rings
answering silence)

& time passes, clinging, impossible beginning
but always having begun & unable
to end but always having ended each step one step more –

26.

You can't so both you & the world must
be broken. The river shallow in late
summer a net of momentary sapphire.

Despite the denial beginning & no slow consideration
why don't they fade away like scars or tail lights trying
not to tell the story again these line breaks –

no metaphor trajectory the gap in the gut
right then – time ends & every voice pauses you
are really listening just that once now –

27.

Even familiar streets which cliff
maybe which animal.
Fox, then, if. Or tourmaline.

Ah, but then we would become more than
modern
———

28.

Nothing new in it but
every pain & every joy & every thought & sigh & everything
unspeakably small or great in your life –

29.

This is the desert. The remnant.
Allow yourself one word a day.
That should be enough.

Even in the city walking
at dawn alone with birdsong
wait I can tell you their names –

30.

With a guidebook open on my street
not me somebody I don't know
where they're going

not that the distance is closed, not that, no question of arrival, union,
     conjunction, merger, no –
distance itself not ending as breathing ends, some day or night, space
between breath & breath, mine & mine, yours & yours, yes, yours & –

31.

Random isn't real enough, or exhibits statistical randomness
while being generated by an entirely deterministic causal process.
What were we talking about? What must they think?

32.

As if homology & diffeomorphism
good words anyway I like them as if
the street were a desert map another desert as if –

33.

Too many ways to divide all these pages & letters & elegies
archaic forms of life unchanged by notebooks or photographs
or beauty unnameable –

the space needs to be filled with quick self not to be
stepped outside. You know what will be outside.
Listening through the open broken window.

34.

Not only the recollection.
The mornings. The days.
The approach or flight of clarity.

No books or too many books,
revised versions.
In every case, empty pages

or the same book on every shelf.
This New Life. La Vita Nova. New Poems.
Did it change?

35.

Circling around something I don't understand or circling
around nothing (& I don't understand that either)
& that's enough. Well, loss is tiresome.

If there were a poem that made this
clear I would copy it here. I can't
say if that's true but I want it to be.

36.

A garden at the valley edge haze not even a dream deceiving
or hope unexamined or narrative only random why count
the words example surplus meaning memory I have too much.

Perhaps no book at all no instructions explanation no real
reason to turn the page nothing at all useful like how
to rid an hour of moths or paint a perfect straight edge.

In the next room someone reading stage directions
trying to name the scene familiar foreign
always even what comes next is far away.

37.

Left-behind voices continue after you explaining every step using
the proper word for every colour. Crimson & saffron predominate.
Once this is done another page morning nothing new here move
   along.

This idea tradition, well there are metaphysical poems & lyric,
the place of human beings in the universe or the lack. Mountains
& huddled knees on the sidewalk leaning back against cold concrete.

38.

Not as if starting an inventory like Perec
(notepad, pencil, stack of dishes, gloves, the cat)
(again I'm lying) but overlap or fold or

I haven't understood a thing.
Heard what I wanted flowers I don't know.
Word cuttings in knotted lines & gaps.

39.

The space needs to be filled with quick self not to be
stepped outside. You know what will be outside.
Listening

temptation, contemplation, beginning, & having to repeat
not having recognized the first inner radiance which would have been
    the best thing
cooling into winter's pure illusory body no different no better not
    driven by geometry or narrative sky –

Portraits of strangers just waking. Self-portraits, asleep.
Bedclothes clenched in which radiance & emptiness are indivisible.
Do you deserve this? The wrong question. Almost-shattered glass.

40.

Portraits in which radiance & emptiness are indivisible.
Shattering the wrong glass
nothing settled clarifies mirrored indications.

Random isn't snow on the ground now. Stop
right there slowly. No two performances
the same lateness always somewhat amid but then

sometimes the form which way the line
swoops is most important. At the end of the other
day nighthawks. Too definite, certain, road or radio noise.

41.

Not like waking up you're outside, there was no door but there's wind
    the smell of green.
Did you do anything different? I don't remember. Still have brown toast
    & jam for breakfast, strong black coffee, & ordinary orange juice.
I don't know if that tall plant growing beside the yellow flowers I don't
    recognize, the one with the jagged leaves & thick stem, is a weed.

42.

Remembering nothing, broken mirrors reflecting blue & a few clouds,
    a simple doorway
or a scrap of language tumbling down the street until it vanishes with
    the ground fog
after dawn, walking in wet meadows just hearing the river we haven't
    reached yet.

Time passes, clinging, impossible beginning
but always having begun & unable
to end but always having ended each step one step more –

43.

Animals & fathers, mothers & friends, lovers, trees, & rosebushes:
Mr. Lincoln, Peace, white York & red Lancaster all history & quote
   some proper English poet here –
distance dimming into shadow, detail becoming shadow. Some
   memories maybe.

44.

This is the desert. The remnant.
Allow yourself one word a day.
That should be enough.

45.

Even in the city walking
at dawn alone with birdsong
wait I can tell you their names.

46.

No ocean here, no mountain, no desert for that matter. Passerby
    reflected
in the windows of the house across the street. The quiet street now
at the heart of this unconcealed & made strange only by omission

circling around something I don't understand or circling
around nothing (& I don't understand that either)
& that's enough. Well, loss is tiresome yes every day.

Outside or alone expecting nothing even wanting nothing
is that true? Usually quiet here & no still point or
escape until they're dull enough every day.

47.

Poetry worth almost nothing its obligations anyway as if spoken &
    speaker could be
separated as if there were a Poem & no answering silence listening in
emptiness the same time it's emptiness saying all this again to make it
    more radiant –

48.

Rework this as there's no joy here
& not enough voices no long poem containing
any vision or revision of history –

49.

Not only the mornings. Not only the days.
Not only the recollection. Not only the paths.
Not only the breathing clarity or the approach of sleep.

The room is empty vocabulary unconfined & pretense
of constraint abandoned our exquisite embroidered equations
growing beyond anything we would choose to wear.

Not haunted nor ruined nor past, lost, not at all but scattered from
the very first day or night or border on insensible imperfection
as though I wanted a complete theory of correspondences.

50.

So the leaves drifting from the trees
in this extended summer the future
will be more of this –

51.

Never done ending even I can't find the beginning
tangle of red tangle black white sky blue blown leaves petals
convention.

If this is repeated it is not repeated exactly decoration a different voice
   & not my voice
from the next room or outside the door the voice of the wind
   change that
another time uncertain past or future fractionally familiar even if I will
   have to rework this –

52.

That there is a gap & you can cross it.
A beauty gap, or a death gap. Pain gap.
Interval or chasm or gulf or refusal maybe better, or parentheses.

Not only the mornings. Not only the days.
Not only the recollection. Not only the paths.
Not only the breathing clarity or the approach of sleep.

53.

Consumed / as a flame consumes
as a flame consumes
as fire / consumes

I can't write what I really can't.
Remember leave things out I am like bees.
That's the real thing is what I said I said.

54.

Can memory be present memory turning
the line rewritten the line rewritten
vision & revision of –

The first time you read those words
they seem extraordinary perhaps
they are.

55.

Three days later gold & silver staff blooming
red flowers twisting round someone's hand
petals falling on the white stone floor

too quickly & neither flawed rage nor consolation will
change a thing nor does it matter what you sing
or if it's beautiful. There it is. Stained upholstery.

56.

I know I'm repeating myself repeating so this new life begins when
walking away from reawakened awareness or obsession or mirrored
not joy just ordinary waking outside memory exists sometimes okay

maybe nothing is broken or ever was a pause an interval a rest
& start again nothing
is it there's only one thing to say but again & again?

The space needs to be filled with quick self not to be
stepped outside. You know what will be outside.
Listening through the open broken window.

57.

Time passes, clinging, impossible beginning
but always having begun & unable
to end but always having ended each step one step more –

A garden at the valley edge haze not even a dream deceiving
or hope unexamined or narrative only random why count
the words example surplus meaning memory I have too much.

Something like breathing the wavelength changes.
The world comes in all of the world.
Plants on the balcony tree in the field.

58.

Disappointing looking back on old love wondering how not to fall
into the false logic of narration this then that to keep
an eye on the scraps as they circle in the wind some will be lost.

59.

Reasonably constant without regard to recognize
pure surface only audience the border to cross unguarded
& that equanimity the dead possess.

60.

Portraits of strangers just waking. Self-portraits, asleep.
Bedclothes clenched in which radiance & emptiness are indivisible.
You deserve this, the almost-shattered glass.

Rework this as there's no joy here
& not enough voices no long poem containing
history –

with a guidebook open on my street
not me somebody I don't know
where they're going.

61.

A frame around life drawing
how the swoop of those lines caught
that glance exactly that can't be ignored

those almost infinitely blue what
does that even mean
almost infinitely –

62.

Like rain, or snow, or lightning, or
the reconstructed track of decaying cosmic rays
never having done this yet.

Start again continuing. Repeat myself.
Or not exactly
when really it's just that beside this –

63.

Ah, but then we would become more than
modern, & death
always so contemporary.

64.

Not that the distance is closed, not that, no question of arrival, union,
     conjunction, merger, no –
distance itself not ending as breathing ends, some day or night, space
between breath & breath, mine & mine, yours & yours, yes, yours & –

with a guidebook open on my street
not me somebody I don't know
where they're going.

65.

That there is a gap & you can cross it.
A beauty gap, or a death gap. Pain gap.
Interval or chasm or gulf or refusal maybe better, or parentheses.

Animals & fathers, mothers & friends, lovers, trees, & rose bushes:
Mr. Lincoln, Peace, white York & red Lancaster all history & quote
    some proper English poet here –
distance dimming into shadow, detail becoming shadow. Some
    memories maybe.

66.

Something like breathing the wavelength changes.
The world comes in all of the world.
Plants on the balcony tree in the field.

Like rain, or snow, or lightning, or
the reconstructed track of decaying cosmic rays
never having done this yet.

Literature piles up to be set aside,
spurious politics & careerism, but the
light, the light, past the first radiance second & the clouds –

67.

Dimly not keeping time winding down or burning out
disappointment to be rebuilt as philosophy perhaps
realization or actualization the fundamental inexplicable
  experienced –

even if some of them are singing
& some lines might have been
deleted.

68.

No need to start. Too much quiet.
When could you take one step forward
without thinking

nothing new in it but
every pain & every joy & every thought & sigh & everything
unspeakably small or great in your life.

Past unravelled though text
remains, read, reread, uncertain
how the one who wrote managed –

69.

Every difference radiating from the same dark fathering
in inconclusive trajectory. From this life no other.
No assembly of fragments because they aren't parts of anything.

70.

I haven't understood a thing.
Heard what I wanted flowers I don't know.
Word cuttings in knotted lines & gaps.

71.

Not like waking up you're outside, there was no door but there's wind
the smell of green.
Did you do anything different? I don't remember. Still have brown
toast & jam for breakfast, strong black coffee, & ordinary orange
juice.
I don't know if that tall plant growing beside the yellow flowers I don't
recognize, the one with the jagged leaves & thick stem, is a weed.

Not only the mornings. Not only the days.
Not only the recollection. Not only the paths.
Not only the breathing clarity or the approach of sleep.

72.

Every difference radiating from the same dark fathering
in inconclusive trajectory. From this life no other.
No assembly of fragments because they aren't parts of anything

never done ending even I can't find the beginning
tangle of red tangle black white sky blue blown leaves petals
convention.

73.

Random isn't snow on the ground now. Stop
right there slowly. No two performances
the same lateness always somewhat amid but then

if this is repeated it is not repeated exactly decoration a different voice
    & not my voice
from the next room or outside the door the voice of the wind
    change that
another time uncertain past or future fractionally familiar even if I will
    have to rework this.

Left behind voices continue after you explaining every step using
the proper word for every colour. Crimson & saffron predominate.
Once this is done another page morning nothing new here move
    along.

74.

Consumed / as a flame consumes
as a flame consumes
as fire / consumes –

An ecstasy never felt.
The pattern, repeated, mechanical.
I thought it would all stop wrong.

The room is empty vocabulary unconfined & pretense
of constraint abandoned our exquisite embroidered equations
growing beyond anything we would choose to wear.

75.

Too quickly & neither flawed rage nor consolation will
change a thing nor does it matter what
or if it's beautiful. There it is.

76.

Random isn't real enough, or exhibits statistical randomness
while being generated by an entirely deterministic causal process.
What were we talking about? What must they think?

As if homology & diffeomorphism
good words anyway I like them as if
the street were a desert map another desert as if –

The book of landscape or the other one
book of feeling, book of time
& the end of time nothing written down.

77.

Perhaps no book at all no instructions explanation no real
reason to turn the page nothing at all useful like how
to rid an hour of moths or paint a perfect grey edge.

A garden at the valley edge haze not even a dream deceiving
or hope unexamined or narrative only random why count
the words example surplus meaning memory I have too much.

78.

Random isn't real enough, or exhibits statistical randomness
while being generated by an entirely deterministic causal process.
What were we talking about? What must they think?

Tempting to say it all again.
Will that help.
Art or grander thievery.

79.

To pare or pass this down to pages & pages of
not stopping & how much can I circle cross
out –

I wonder if there will be voices. The books of etiquette seem to be out
    of date.
Maybe I could ask for a letter of introduction like Jack Spicer write it
    myself.
I dreamed I saw St. Augustine. Not really.

80.

Despite the denial beginning & no slow consideration
why don't they fade away like scars or tail lights trying
not to tell the story again these line breaks don't twist enough –

three days later gold & silver staff blooming
red flowers twisting round the hand
petals falling on someone's white stone floor.

81.

Even space not space & time not time
just missing. Moments & places just missing.
Wood & paper reminders. The pattern breaking up.

Don't mess this up I said watching
the waves crest dark & light high & low in & out
of phase. It's too simple.

82.

Perhaps no book at all no instructions explanation no real
reason to turn the page nothing at all useful like how
to rid an hour of moths or paint a perfect straight edge.

"Fling the emptiness out of your arms," he says
& that's well said. But what does that leave you embracing?
"Ah, they only hide their loneliness in one another."

83.

Perhaps no book at all no instructions explanation no real
reason to turn the page nothing at all useful like how
to rid an hour of moths or paint a black perfect edge.

My illness to be alone & not enough words
possibility of bright understanding complicity.
Only the reaching over broken lines, & lines.

84.

To pare or pass this down not stopping
& how much can I call
vision & revision, pages & pages of –

85.

To pare or pass this down to pages & pages of
not stopping & how much can I circle cross
out –

too many ways to divide all these pages & letters & elegies
archaic forms of life unchanged by notebooks or photographs
or beauty unnameable recognized –

Portraits of strangers just waking. Self-portraits, asleep.
Bedclothes clenched in which radiance & emptiness are indivisible.
The wrong question. Almost-shattered glass.

86.

The sea at dawn in black & white. The waves
move an individual wave is difficult to distinguish.
Use a sieve or comb, they say. One of those egg-yolk things, a gateway,
    or a quantum switch.

Disappointing looking back on old love wondering how not to fall
into the false logic of narration this then that to keep
an eye on the scraps as they circle in the wind some will be lost. That's
    good.

87.

Every difference radiating from the same dark fathering
in inconclusive trajectory. From this life no other.
No assembly of fragments because they aren't parts of anything.

Dimly not keeping time winding down or burning out
disappointment to be rebuilt as philosophy perhaps
realization or actualization the fundamental inexplicable
   experienced –

88.

Nothing new in it but
every pain & every joy & every thought & sigh & everything
unspeakably small or great in your life

even this spider & this moonlight
between the trees
even this moment & –

Time passes, clinging, impossible beginning
but always having begun & unable
to end but always having ended each step one step more –

89.

Silence. Or strawberries. At least breathing
& the noise one afternoon makes remember
reflection didn't break the mirror.

90.

Never done ending even I can't find the beginning
tangle of red tangle black white sky blue blown leaves petals
convention

consumed / as a flame consumes
as a flame consumes
as fire / consumes –

91.

The legend is too big. A ruin, or a relic, then reading the castle still
     stands at Duino.
Taking dictation from those who would destroy you & then they stop.
Imperfection of wisdom. Its attraction. You know the rest.

92.

If there were a poem that made this
clear I would copy it here. I can't
say if that's true but I want it to be.

Consumed / as a flame consumes
as a flame consumes
as fire / consumes –

The everyday again the everyday.
I don't care about Rilke's angels anymore, I said. Who does?
Sweep the floor. Put away the books. Fill a glass with water.

93.

No correct one. A branching
tangled tree overgrown with vines, no line
breaks now. Monochrome, only edges.

Not that the distance is closed, not that, no question of arrival, union,
    conjunction, merger, no –
distance itself not ending as breathing ends, some day or night, space
between breath & breath, mine & mine, yours & yours, yes –

94.

No need to start. Too much quiet.
When could you take one step forward
without thinking

no books or too many books,
revised versions.
In every case, empty pages.

95.

Start again continuing. Repeat myself.
Or not exactly
when really it's just that beside this –

96.

With a guidebook open on my street
not me somebody I don't know
where they're going

to pare or pass this down to pages & pages of
not stopping & how much can I circle cross
out –

97.

Even in the city walking
at dawn alone with birdsong
wait –

Past nothing to do with no history no tradition no wonder
I believe in nothing but it is possible to want
to believe at the same time confusing just a little.

98.

I haven't understood a thing.
Heard what I wanted flowers I don't know.
Word cuttings in knotted lines & gaps.

99.

Left-behind voices continue after you explaining every step using
the proper word for every colour. Crimson & saffron predominate.
Once this is done another page morning nothing new here move
  along.

100.

Outside or alone expecting nothing even wanting nothing
is that true? Usually quiet here & no still point or
escape until they're dull enough every day.

101.

Throwing rocks at what is it downed owl or rabbit or cat
at the back of the schoolyard ditch white with snow & dark
woods beyond look blood it's not moving now –

102.

Repeating myself again
disorder, sorrow, & joy unevenly
distributed causation –

103.

The book of landscape or the other one
book of feeling, book of time
& the end of time nothing written down.

No need to start. Too much quiet.
When could you take one step forward
without thinking envy privilege tradition?

104.

Circling around something I don't understand or circling
around nothing (& I don't understand that either)
& that's enough. Well, loss is tiresome yes every day.

Disappointing looking back on old love wondering how not to fall
into the false logic of narration this then that to keep
an eye on the scraps as they circle in the wind some will be lost.

105.

The everyday again the everyday.
I don't care about Rilke's angels anymore, I said. Do you?
Sweep the floor. Put away the books. Fill a glass with water.

Not haunted nor ruined nor past, lost, not at all but scattered from
the very first day or night or border on insensible imperfection
as though I wanted a complete theory of correspondences.

Perhaps no book at all no instructions explanation no real
reason to turn the page nothing at all useful like how
to rid an hour of moths or paint a perfect straight edge.

106.

Ah, but then we would become more than
modern, & death
always so contemporary.

107.

The everyday again the everyday.
I don't care about anyone's angels anymore, I said.
Sweep the floor. Put away the books. Fill a glass with water.

Empty rage cloud. Desire wind. Moth cloud.
Opening this door will sound the alarm.
Only that.

Every difference radiating from the same dark fathering
in inconclusive trajectory. From this life no other.
No assembly of fragments because they aren't parts of anything.

108.

But whose words anyway?
Not much art in them.
And if some sense made it through regardless?

109.

That there is a gap & you can cross it.
A beauty gap, or a death gap. Pain gap.
Interval or chasm or gulf or refusal maybe better, or parentheses.

Perhaps no book at all no instructions explanation no real
reason to turn the page nothing at all useful like how
to rid an hour of moths or paint a perfect straight

undistracted no one cross that out no
action is destroyed & choice
later irrelevant to later –

110.

Literature piles up to be set aside,
spurious politics & careerism, but the
light, the light, past the first radiance second & the clouds –

too many ways to divide all these pages & letters & elegies
archaic forms of life unchanged by notebooks or photographs
or beauty unnameable recognized –

111.

Sometimes the form which way the line
swoops is most important. At the end of the other
day nighthawks. Too definite, certain, road or radio noise.

Not like waking up you're outside, there was no door but there's wind
    the smell of green.
Did you do anything different? I don't remember. Still have brown
    toast & jam for breakfast, strong black coffee, & ordinary orange
    juice.
I don't know if that tall plant growing beside the yellow flowers I don't
    recognize, the one with the jagged leaves & thick stem, is a weed.

Something like breathing the wavelength changes.
The world comes in all of the world.
Plants on the balcony tree in the field.

112.

Undistracted no one cross that out no
action is destroyed & choice
later irrelevant to later –

The everyday again the everyday.
Don't anymore, I said.
Sweep the floor. Put away the books. Fill a glass with water.

113.

All-original melancholy
fresh as the song you never heard
but you heard it here

like analogue noise in several voices no counterpoint or plan
no melody or purpose different kinds of paper now listen
what you feel isn't interesting there's two hours of daylight left –

114.

As if cohomology & invariants
good words anyway I like them as if
the street were a desert map another desert as if –

even this spider & this moonlight
between the trees
even this moment &

the same book on every shelf.
This New Life. La Vita Nova. New Poems.
Something like that.

115.

The language spoken across the street. Fire
just below the breastbone every breath too aware
of breathing. Fingers cramped, their hold too tight.

Left-behind voices continue after you explaining every step using
the proper word for every colour. Crimson & saffron predominate.
Once this is done another page morning nothing new here move
    along.

116.

Despite the denial beginning & no slow consideration
why don't they fade away like scars or tail lights trying
not to tell the story again these line breaks

not haunted nor ruined nor past, lost, not at all but scattered from
the very first day or night or border on insensible imperfection
as though I wanted a complete theory of correspondences –

117.

My illness to be alone & not enough words
possibility of bright understanding complicity.
Only the reaching over broken lines, & lines.

Like rain, or snow, or lightning, or
the reconstructed track of decaying cosmic rays
never having done this yet.

118.

No ocean here, no mountain, no desert for that matter. Passerby
    reflected
in the windows of the house across the street. The quiet street now
at the heart of this unconcealed & made strange only by omission.

Literature piles up to be set aside,
spurious politics & careerism, but the
light, the light, past the first radiance second & the clouds –

119.

This idea tradition, well there are metaphysical poems & lyric,
the place of human beings in the universe or the lack. Mountains
& huddled knees on the sidewalk leaning back against cold concrete.

120.

A few words stolen from a stranger ill-met in early fog,
no story at all, even repetition no better self-deception
rewriting the same pages again.

PART THREE

BEGINNING AGAIN & AGAIN IS A NATURAL THING EVEN WHEN THERE IS A SERIES

1.

Or the wind
crowded with voice a matter
of taking dictation, translating

the only one
who knows that language &
recalls sublime moments thought

swerved at the edge of.
All the seas below, & rushing.
No hierarchy of oceans.

2.

A brief glimpse past the door
closing behind someone leaving,
waking up from another library dream

the same book on every shelf.
This New Life. La Vita Nova. New Poems.
Something like that. Dark oak clouds

blowing through the strange empty crowded room.
Lost in their overcoats at every table,
muttering to themselves. Warm grey wool.

3.

Piles & stacks & scraps
broken clay pots
describing things that happened

or could have
a sudden gust of wind
paper blue sky & geometry

mountain or flat land
industrial park
a red scarf –

4.

This new life confessional
or abstract, deep or
shallow unrhymed

beginning or end as if
unscattered & whole when
broken – there's no repair.

Words catch & snag & shatter.
The silence after neither
redemption nor respite.

5.

To want to pour jewels out
on the sidewalk but who will see them
death will see them knowing

the words without reading
being the words I can't recite.
A prescribed litany names

of angels or hours in definite order
implicate order each touching
the other infinitely far from the other.

6.

No longer travelling, at home
both the east wall & the west have windows
covered by tangled vines.

Beyond one, a silver mountain.
Beyond the other, a towering iron cliff.
At sunrise in slant light recalling shallow sleep

on fast trains in the past I sit
seeing them both, the empty room
awaiting half a phrase.

7.

But whose words anyway?
Not much art in them.
And if some sense made it through regardless?

Orpheus coming up the subway stairs
Spring Street again, raining again, still seeing
Eurydice fixed

in imagination unchanging & eternal –
Always at the edge of ending endlessly.
Of course you have to change the names.

8.

Temptation to escape into
ornament, archive embroidery
the brocade of sky or palladium.

Places spread out
a cloak or a bedsheet.
Like grey wool a bit

moth-eaten, crumbling into white.
Where did they come from & where
did they go.

9.

The simple turn
off the path this time
hillside to mountainside

grey clouds pleated
far above blue but still
the simple urge

to lie down pillowed
on stone wait
for nightfall, stars.

10.

Right now recedes to now
left over. In this moment decades
half a conversation under

machines & machines & children & wind
in the leaves. Bicycle. Dog. Cicada.
No pattern. Black. Red. Black.

Perfect posture. No scent. No smoke.
Cool enough in the shade.
Table green silver graffiti. Aluminum.

11.

Past unravelled though text
remains, read, reread, uncertain
how the one who wrote managed

now, unclear how the clarity
that seems was, the smoke
from too many bonfires of books between

us, what's past is past is –
Somewhere I lost track, blacked
out. An anaesthesia, cold slippage –

12.

Light fading
& rain again, light
rain asking if I

will fade into weather
well we all will.
Is that what this is

when you can say the light
has faded completely
rain continues.

13.

Looked at in the absence of the future
there is only history, & all the names
worn from gravestones by weather

or perhaps that's just a particularly regular
slab of stone. Quarried, never used.
Spotted by lichen, etched by rain.

Looked at in the absence of the future
can memory be present memory turning
the line rewritten the line rewritten –

14.

To undo these messengers
who see everything who
remember nothing

who speak in silence
or rumoured thunder never
heard here, imagined maybe

& how to undo
imagination
or lost desire no desire –

15.

Isn't lost twilight
grey purple damson night
later

barely remembering
what
isn't remembered

we didn't write letters then
lines getting shorter & shorter everything
touching –

16.

Past perfected, well, completed
perhaps only by death but still
or only quiet those years

without society or solitude
looking out at imagined
mountains imagined wild imagined

paths & just a brief glimpse really
going nowhere alone or always alone
today cloud banners & clear keen light.

17.

Let's say a book of hours
this hour fog
just above the trees beyond

oak trees past
the cemetery weeded
Saturday by the townspeople.

"A broken bundle of mirrors," Pound wrote
but a different mirror
& by the bridge, convex, diverging.

18.

Another tower far from the sea
no waves breaking, no wings
overhead or seabirds' cries

no sails to watch for
white, black, red –
whose voice? A confusion

of voices, mirrored sound unsourced
& unrecognized. There should be
a set text, an order, I said.

19.

Left with the decay of
rattle of indrawn breath over
thick air, cold air

to reduce to ashes, every
communication disconnected
no numbers random numbers

zeros & ones with equal
probability –
Was that it I've forgotten.

20.

Repeating myself again
not the taste remembered .
but the tasting

some ground pepper
some coarse salt
dove in the tree by the door

laurel, maybe
bay laurel, sweet bay, bay
waves breaking below not here –

21.

Because you want to look back
from the end & see the whole thing.
Sense completeness. Pattern. Order even in

disorder, sorrow & joy unevenly
distributed causation
clotted with regret

coincidence not to be ignored
not the same thing, or poetry
the right words stretched beyond –

22.

Can't say anymore
or exhausted by saying
again emptied out

there is no void.
Vision & revision of
creation & annihilation

is this too much
language.
Was that it I've forgotten.

23.

The first time you read those words
they seem extraordinary perhaps
they are or were

& in time
the experience is everyday
or they tell you it is

if clearly seen
flowers & trees & dust
on the books, the bookshelves –

24.

The neighbour's mailbox across the road
old postman's shuffle as he
makes his way up the street

in the early afternoon rain.
Any season clearly seen
& no message in the seeing

no messengers
the empty details at arm's length
entropy when this book is full.

25.

Start again continuing. Repeat myself.
Or not exactly
when really it's just this

beside that the same way this isn't
this new life every moment not
news a clip a loop gli/itched apocalypse

empty structure ritual
to move through to
live –

26.

No beginning again always mislaying some
capability or object pen keys credit card
phone despite the memory of each

scrap of paper scattered on this one
a way of talking about death
without using the word

as if feeling could be replaced
with wanting to know for certain if
something has been left out.

27.

Only the wind letting loose
repair & destruction leaving all
the rest in short phrases stretched

across attention's sharp edges as
fast clouds cataract the sky
the acid ocean exploding against its

dark mathematics in every beauty
or encrypted inevitable sublime
heart clenched thought of numbers.

28.

At the edge of unthinking
no turns this algorithm deepens
& throws fire back at us some pieces

bigger than others past
the yellow sign & the black curve left
the wooden floor (pale maple) reflects

the windows at the far end of the long room
as if the unbroken teleology of architecture
dissolved into unwanted definition.

29.

Cause & shadow of effect & no end
to rehearsing difference & sameness
times without time for truth or consideration

some facts deleted but not changed as
the confined year finishes with a cold breeze not even
filling the page much less the heart

wind from the southeast constant meaning
there could be rain again tomorrow
clouds racing grey weather noted.

30.

Sometimes a summary
is possible. You know it's coming.
Sometimes the neighbour's roses

spill over the fence. That's okay. You can
grow out of desire. The empty bowl
doesn't need to be filled with petals.

The view of the mountains doesn't need
to be framed by the garden.
There doesn't need to be a garden.

31.

Everything in this garden is purple
or pale yellow. You didn't need
to know that. It's a pure gift

or distraction & impure.
Lines written here remembering
other gardens every one recovered

from a different chaos
or imposed, unknowing, even
here, the deep tangle of this (every) city.

32.

As for purity, or clarity, form, the real thing
you have to be willing to throw it away
"the poet's mission [ha!] & the demands of life"

this life

the cat sleeping in the sunshine on the writing table
the walk to the bookshop through the park
unfallen leaves (late for that) something new

by Lyn Hejinian & what to make of it:
Irrational elegies, she says, because loss doesn't make
sense leaving logic to line breaks & stanzas then –

33.

If I wake before dawn (& old, I often do)
& there are a few stars bright
over the lovely lit towers, monuments

that will come down
in the weather that men
& women & all of us have made

I can only remark the quiet
scattered light. This is not a silent time.
Morning is emptiness. You know the rest.

34.

The house where I'm writing this
a little over a century old.
No waves breaking far below.

No beginning again just
as there's no static between stations just
as there are no stations now no

standing still unless at
the beginning the very beginning
& this is not the beginning again.

35.

And the light?
Dark, dark, they say.
The wooden floor (not a mirror) reflecting

the windows at the far end
of the long room the clouds
beyond grey-blue, or heaven-grey, heart-grey

the wind unbounded now.
Borrowing another poet's words again
only half remembering.

36.

Of course we remember
things differently. The voices
you hear in the bardo

are vague, maybe that's the best
way to put it. But
you strain to make out the words, maybe

you make up the words
& later you remember
what you wanted to hear.

37.

The petals of this week's tulips
scattered on the table & the floor –
sunshine on the stones outside, cause

& effect of shadow. No end
to remembering difference & sameness.
No end to asking

for a simple explanation, the desire
for a simple straight line
from the beginning to the end remains.

38.

That there is a gap & you can cross it.
A beauty gap, or a death gap. Pain gap.
Interval, chasm, gulf, or refusal maybe better, or parentheses.

Still every word
is separated from the word
before & after.

No thought in that gap
but I think it's where we are
alive most particularly.

39.

Mist drifting through the trees
in this wood, not dark, not
light either. Well mapped in places, sure

but trees fall & paths veer.
You could say these are the woods
we come from, populated

with terrors imagined & perpetrated.
Clearing just ahead the path loops & it's lost.
A story you could tell but only the fog listens.

40.

A turning point a point of inflection, reflection
change of season ending beginning
disaffection, abandonment, retreat

Turn a few pages back
Is that a thrush
Is that a kingfisher

The pattern breaking up

A turning point a bifurcation
a decision to be made
a choice

between writing & living
between watching & living
between working & living
between waiting & living
between living & living

SOURCES

As usual these poems incorporate the words of others. Tradition or theft.

The translation of the quotation from Rainer Maria Rilke's "Ninth Elegy" in the epigraph is my own.

The title of the first section, "The foretaste of a vision, but never the vision itself," is a quotation from section 79 of Friedrich Nietzsche's *The Gay Science*, translated by Josefine Nauckhoff.

The title of the second section, "Like the noises alive people wear," is a quotation from Jack Spicer's "A Textbook of Poetry," in *The Heads of the Town up to the Aether*.

The title of the third section, "Beginning again & again is a natural thing even when there is a series," is a quotation from Gertrude Stein's "Composition as Explanation."

There are many quotations buried in the body of the poems. A more or less complete list follows.

PART ONE

"Mountain flowers bloom like brocade, valley streams brimming blue indigo. On the ancient cliff, frigid juniper" is from the *Blue Cliff Record*, case 82, in Thomas Cleary and J.C. Cleary's translation.

"nothing else but a kind of circling" is from Lancelot Andrewes's Ash Wednesday sermon of 1619.

PART TWO

2.2 "Look, I am living" is from my translation of Rilke's "Ninth Elegy."

2.3. "That thing they posted Clark Coolidge wrote"
Unfortunately, I can no longer find the text by Coolidge this refers to. I was sure I had it somewhere.

2.4. "it coolly disdains to destroy you" is from Edward Snow's translation of Rilke's "First Elegy."

2.7. "& not enough voices no long poem containing history"
In his 1934 essay "Date Line" (collected in *Literary Essays of Ezra Pound*), Pound defined an epic as "a poem containing history."

2.9. "Not as if starting an inventory like Perec"
I was thinking of *An Attempt at Exhausting a Place in Paris*, but Georges Perec wrote lots of inventories.

2.14 "beauty is nothing but the beginning of terror" is from Snow's translation of Rilke's "First Elegy."

2.31. "Random isn't real enough, or exhibits statistical randomness"
See en.wikipedia.org/wiki/Pseudorandomness (accessed June 27, 2017).

2.49. "Not only the mornings. Not only the days" is from my translation of Rilke's "Seventh Elegy."

2.55. "Three days later gold & silver staff blooming"
Perhaps a reference to Richard Wagner's *Tannhäuser*, if that has anything to do with this, which it probably doesn't.

2.59. "& that equanimity the dead possess" is from Snow's translation of Rilke's "Fourth Elegy."

2.79 "Maybe I could ask for a letter of introduction like Jack Spicer write it myself."
See the introduction to Spicer's *After Lorca*.

2.82 "Fling the emptiness out of your arms" is from Stephen Mitchell's translation of Rilke's "First Elegy."

2.82 "Ah, they only hide their loneliness in one another" is from William H. Gass's translation of Rilke's "First Elegy."

2.88 "even this spider & this moonlight" is from Nietzsche's *Gay Science*, section 341, translated by Josefine Nauckhoff.

PART THREE

3.6 "Beyond one, a silver mountain. Beyond the other, a towering iron cliff" is a reference to Hakuin's *Poison Blossoms from a Thicket of Thorn*, book nine, section 349, translated by Norman Waddell. Hakuin in turn references a poem by Hanshan, as well as a saying of Haihui Shoudan, which is also quoted in the *Blue Cliff Record*.

3.13 "Looked at in the absence of the future" is from Louise Glück's essay "American Narcissism" (collected in *American Originality: Essays on Poetry*).

3.17 "A broken bundle of mirrors" is from Pound's poem "Near Perigord," found in *A Walking Tour of Southern France: Ezra Pound among the Troubadours* (edited by Richard Sieburth).

3.32 "the poet's mission [ha!] & the demands of life" is a comment on Rilke's life at Duino from Donald Prater's biography, *A Ringing Glass: The Life of Rainer Maria Rilke*.

3.32 "something new by Lyn Hejinian" is *The Unfollowing*, published in 2016.

3.35 "beyond grey-blue, or heaven-grey, heart-grey" references the title poem in Paul Celan's *Sprachgitter*.

ACKNOWLEDGMENTS

Thirty-three of the first forty segments of part two appeared in an earlier version as a chapbook (*Like the noises alive people wear*, above/ground press, 2019). Thanks to rob mclennan for this.

Poem 33 ("If I wake before dawn …") in part three previously appeared in a different form in *G U E S T* 16, "The FANGIRL Issue," edited by Kirby (February 2021).

Gratitude to Catriona Strang and Charles Simard and everyone else at Talonbooks, as well as to Les Smith for the gorgeous cover.

Finally, many thanks to David Bradford, Rose Cullis, Guy Ewing, Doug and Jeannine Friesen, Kirby, and Lisa Robertson for conversation and encouragement in various forms while this was all coming together.

ABOUT THE AUTHOR

R. Kolewe has published three previous collections of poetry, *Afterletters* (Book*hug, 2014), *Inspecting Nostalgia* (Talonbooks, 2017), and *The Absence of Zero* (Book*hug, 2021), as well as several chapbooks. He lives in Toronto.